Yoga of Psychosis

From Sinner to Savior to

Something in Between

By

Anshu Patre

Copyright © 2023 Anshu Patre

All rights reserved....

ISBN: 9798322532408

God

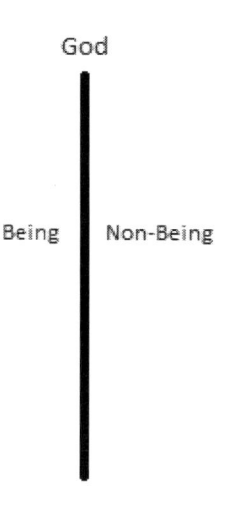

Being | Non-Being

Duality	Nonduality	Duality
Heaven	Utopia	Earth
Father	Children	Mother
Light	Unity	Darkness
Self	Love	Other
East	World Peace	West
Being	Paradox	Non-Being

"Man's consciousness was created to the end that it may (1) recognize its descent from a higher unity; (2) pay due and careful regard to this source; (3) execute its commands intelligently and responsibly; and (4) thereby afford the psyche as a whole the optimum degree of life and development."

– Carl Jung

I did not choose

to be God.

God chose

to be me.

Summary of Book in Pictures

Part 1 — Living in the Culturescape

Step 1 — Brainwashed by the CultureScape

Step 2 — Question the Brules and Master the CultureScape

(Breaking Out of the System....One)

Part 2 — The Awakening

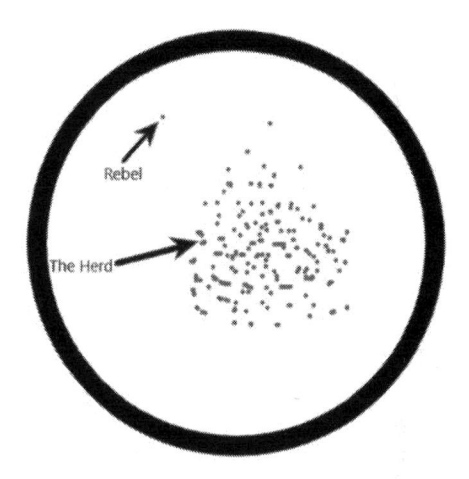

"All thing things that truly matter, beauty, love, creativity, joy, and inner peace arise from beyond the mind." - Eckhart Tolle

Part 3 — Recoding Yourself

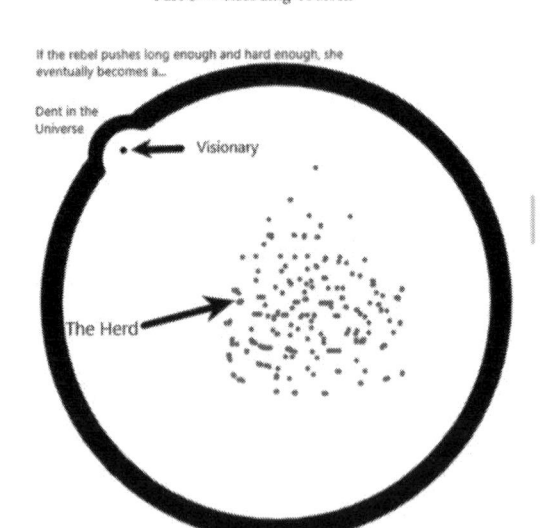

If the rebel pushes long enough and hard enough, she eventually becomes a...

Dent in the Universe

← Visionary

The Herd

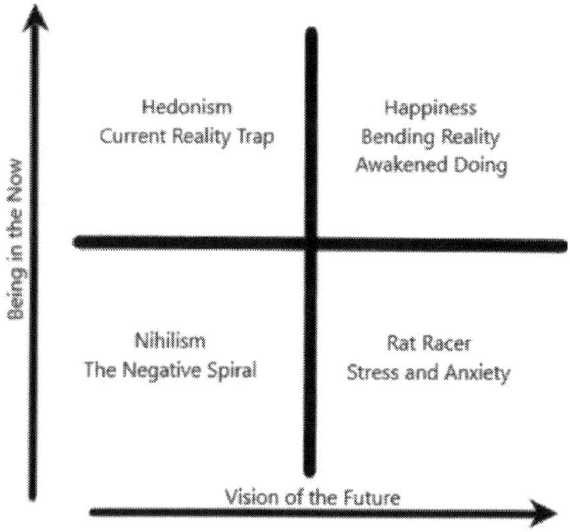
Hedonism
Current Reality Trap
Happiness
Bending Reality
Awakened Doing
Being in the Now
Nihilism
The Negative Spiral
Rat Racer
Stress and Anxiety
Vision of the Future

Part 4 — Changing the World

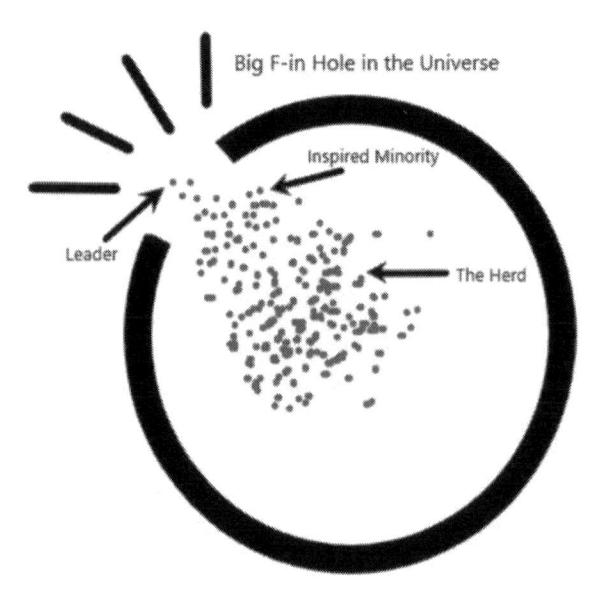

Introduction

As I sit here, meditating in front of the holy mandala in the Yogaville meditation hall, I wonder at the complex threads that tie the past, present, and future together. About twelve years earlier, I had a blissful vision of this same symbol; what Carl Jung calls the archetype of the Self.

Between that past vision and my present state, my life path has been through so many twists and turns that it blows my mind. This body-mind has been through incredible suffering and rapturous joy; through suicidal depression and self-transcendent love. Yet somehow, through all of it, there has been this guiding thread; hidden sometimes, but always present.

Somehow, the inner vision that I had in my twenties has manifested itself in external reality. What happened within me is now happening without. The first book I ever wrote (called the Paradoxical Light) was written of its own accord;

without my conscious choice or consent. It simply rose out of me. It is about the story of civilization and the nature of God.

And most fundamentally, it is about peace, love, and heaven on earth. This Truth has gripped me ever since my first spiritual awakening. I held onto it (or it held onto me) despite all of the hard knocks that life has dealt me. And today, as if by some miracle, the Truth within that book is becoming the Truth of my life. Heaven on earth is now my life.

Today, on a daily basis, I hit states of such joy and wonder that it literally blows my mind. I never knew what happiness was until I left drug addiction behind and came to Yogaville. I write this book and detail my journey in hopes that you, dear reader, can find what I have found; a life that truly matters.

Chapter 1

My childhood was much like many who grow up in middle class suburban America. In fact, I was luckier than most. My house was at the end of a street where another five boys lived. There was Brett, Drew, Jacob, Cole, Kyle and Caleb. We swam in the summer, shot fireworks, played videogames, and every kind of sport.

From what I remember, my early life was pretty amazing. I was mostly happy, relatively popular, and plenty smart. In ninth grade, I had a very hot Indian girlfriend who was two years older than me. (This gave me all sorts of street cred with my friends.)

It was all pretty normal, but things get interesting when it comes to my religious upbringing. My family is Hindu, but my parents sent me to a private Christian school when I turned ten. I went to church on Friday and temple on Sunday.

As an unreflective child who was more interested in video games than Reality, I did not question any of it. I was just as swept up by the joyous songs to Jesus as I was moved by the Hindu bhajans to Krishna. The music of both cultures elevated my heart and soul.

I remember a few moments of awareness in an otherwise blissfully ignorant childhood. One day, when I was walking to church, I had the thought, "Oh, my thoughts occur in time." With that simple insight, I felt this sense of pure joy and inner peace. That day in particular, I especially enjoyed the Christian choir music.

Another time, when I was in Hindu temple, I went into this state of hyper conscious presence as the entire group chanted, "Oooommmmmm" together. Our voices were so harmonized that I still remember the sacred power of that moment. I don't remember much of what was said in temple, and I only remember one sermon that the pastor gave us during church.

He told us a story about how some kids one day smeared paint all over his daughter's car; about how he didn't know if he could ever get it off. And then, searching his garage, he found a tool that was made for the exact purpose of removing paint from cars. It had been sitting there unused for years, but ready to do its job.

And then, for some strange reason, while delivering the final lines of his sermon, the pastor looked at me. I remember seeing God in his eyes. He said something like, "Just like that tool, we are all made for a special purpose. Our job is to find out what it is."

Summary of the Rest of the Book

- Lots of Drugs
- Experience of Transcendent Bliss and the Archetype of the Self
- Meditation, Spiritual Reading and Writing
- Disconnection and Inner Alienation
- Psychotic Savior Complex and Psychedelics
- More Drugs
- More Drugs
- Go Homeless and Find Psychedelics Again
- More Drugs
- Find Yogaville
- Start Meditating a Lot

- Integrate Spiritual Experience
- Hit Super Joyful Love States
- Find Vipassana and Yoga
- And Here I am

Chapter 2

As I moved into adolescence and college, the existence of God became an increasingly foreign and hard to believe idea. To my superficial thinking, the reality of evil and human suffering basically destroyed any belief in God. I never imagined for a second that God could exist as a foundation of Love beyond the opposites of good and evil.

And so I moved into my college years with a firmly scientific and materialistic mindset. I always had some sense of compassion for others, so I wanted to become a doctor like my parents. And yet, on the other hand, I was always this carefree and unthinking youth.

Initially, I resisted the urge to smoke pot whenever it was offered to me, but soon the peer pressure overwhelmed any sense of personal and moral autonomy. A psychologist might say that my conscious ego was taken over by my unconscious evolutionary drives to form social bonds with friends.

Initially, weed was just a way to hang out with friends, but soon I discovered that it also gave me a kick ass high. What Sigmund Freud calls the id figures powerfully into this phase of my life; the part of our psyche that seeks pleasure. The id is unchecked by social or external reality, moving instead in the realms of fantasy, dreams and wish-fulfillment.

Very quickly, the id within me gained control over my life, and I soon stopped caring about grades. I skipped classes to get high. In order to pass, I started taking Adderall (a stimulant cousin of methamphetamine) in order to pull all-nighters before the test. Initially, this was the major reason that I took it. But as I fell further into the tentacles of addiction, Adderall quickly turned into a party drug. I would use it to stay up all night clubbing with friends. Eventually, the party stopped and the addiction turned into weekends of taking Adderall, smoking weed, playing violent video games, and watching pornography for several hours without pause.

Sex and violence have existed within the human psyche for eons. (Such drives have been papered over by the social niceties of modern civilization and the arrogant illusions that many people hold, thinking that they are somehow "above" these primordial impulses.) Little did I know at the time that this behavior was the result of the instinctual, pleasure seeking, fantasy driven unconscious having its way with me. Much of this activity happened out without my conscious consent. It was an extreme variation of the behavior of my ancestors for tens of thousands of years.

"Consciousness is a very recent acquisition of nature, and it is still in an "experimental" state. It is frail, menaced by specific dangers, and easily injured." - Carl Jung

These forces long predate the emergence of human consciousness. They originate in the unconscious, and the drugs simply unlocked this deeply buried, this hidden and latent desire within me. And yet, to make things more complicated, my first experiences with Adderall were not simply physically exhilarating, they also opened up a moral dimension within my soul. The first time that I took amphetamines, I was with a few college friends, and I still remember the feeling of being so completely overwhelmed with love for the world and for my friends in the room.

Nevertheless, these higher emotions quickly gave way to the depravity hidden within the depths of my being. I was consumed by the dark side and my own selfish hedonism. But even in those days of mindless video games and sex, I remember this one moment, which really showed me who I truly was beneath the drug addiction.

When I was high on drugs, I remember playing this video game called, Fable II, for several hours without pause. As you go through the game, you make a series of choices that determine the moral fate of your character and the destiny of the universe. You determine whether you become a tyrant or savior of the mythical land of Albion.

For the entire time that I played the game, I simply made decisions that maximized my character's skill set and progress. Sometimes, I would be good if it served my progress. Other times, I would be evil. This meant that, as I approached the end of the game, my character fell firmly in the grey zone; not too good and not too evil.

Nevertheless, I remember having a spiritual moment of quiet reflection at the end of the game. I beat the evil king and was given three choices:

(1) The Greedy Option: Take the tyrants' place as lord of the earth.

(2) The Middle Path: Be king, but be a good king.

(3) The Saintly Road: Give all of your power and wealth away to serve the people.

For whatever reason, after thinking for a few moments, I choose option three. I didn't consider it much at the time, but, looking back, it really told me something about my character. Even high on drugs, I chose the path of selfless service to mankind (in a video game).

Nevertheless, these moments of selfless love were few and far between. The drugs had all but taken over my life. Over time, I began to lose friends. I smoked so much weed that I could barely function or carry a conversation. My grades suffered terribly, and by my second year of college, I was on the fast track to self-destruction.

And this, my friends, is when God entered my life.

Chapter 3

"Reality sees to it that the peaceful cycle of egocentric ideas is constantly interrupted by ideas with a strong feeling-tone, that is, by affects. A situation threatening danger pushes aside the tranquil play of ideas and puts in their place a complex of other ideas with a very strong feeling-tone. The new complex then crowds everything else into the background." - Carl Jung

By sophomore year of college, my life had all but fallen apart. Of course, I was more or less unaware of it until one fateful day when I was at my friends' house. We were smoking weed and listening to music (as usual). I took a hit of some hash and sat back while the song, Here We Go by Bassnectar, was playing on the speakers. For some reason, when the song hit its climax, I went into this state of pure joy. It was so powerful that I literally lost consciousness of outer reality.

While in this blissful daze, I said goodbye to my friends and left. I got into my car and started driving down the street when another vision rocked my world. It lasted a few seconds, but here is what happened:

Short Version

Symbols of the opposites of the universe spiraled closer and closer to the center of a circle of light, culminating in a vision of nondualistic unity alongside the experience of timeless and transcendent bliss.

Long Version

(1) I was seized by this subtle feeling of happiness. In my mind's eye, I saw the symbolic image of the feminine.

(2) The happiness turned to joy. The image transformed into the symbol of the masculine.

(3) The joy grew stronger. The symbolic image of Mother Earth appeared.

(4) The joy turned into bliss as all of human history and civilization unraveled before my eyes.

(5) The images came too quickly to tell, spiraling closer and closer to the center.

(6) As I approached the center, the bliss became indescribable and unbearable.

(7) I entered the Center and lost all consciousness of outer reality as well as all consciousness of self. I completely disappeared into a vortex of pure light and I don't remember anything after this point.

I came out of the experience a changed man. Nevertheless, the change was slow, painstaking, and mostly happened without my conscious involvement. I did not (and still do not completely) understand what happened at the time, but after a decade of spiritual growth and reading, I now look at the spiritual experience through the lens of Jungian psychology.

Numinous (adjective) – filled with the presence of divinity, a spiritual essence capable of engendering deep and intense emotions or experiences.

"Numinosity, however, is wholly outside conscious volition, for it transports the subject into the state of rapture, which is a state of will-less surrender." - Carl Jung

To summarize, this spiritual experience was the numinous Self (a central archetype of the collective unconscious) erupting into waking consciousness (most likely) due to a temporary dissolution of boundaries between my conscious and unconscious psyche. To explain this prior sentence, I will take you, reader, into the foundational ideas of Carl Jung's psychology.

And probably, the most fundamental idea of Jung's is the distinction between conscious and unconscious. In what follows, I would ask you, reader, to not simply read and intellectually understand what consciousness is and what the unconscious is. Instead, try to grasp the lived reality of these forces within your psyche.

"There is no consciousness without discrimination of opposites." - Carl Jung

The simplest way to grasp the reality of the conscious vs. unconscious psyche is to enquire into the nature of the self. Ask yourself: Who am I? What am I? Look deeply into the reality machine that is you. You are existence itself. This awareness can be likened to the light. The ego, or little self, is the center of this field of awareness, maintaining a stable sense of personal identity and our awareness of being. By its very nature, consciousness is one sided because its scope is limited and therefore its attention is selective.

Meanwhile, the biggest idea of depth psychology is that there are parts of "you" that "you" are not aware of. This is the dark. First, there is the personal unconscious, or the activities of your individual psyche that you are not aware of. The personal unconscious, most significantly, includes everything that you involuntarily and spontaneously desire, think, feel, and remember without being consciously aware of it. It is a profound realization when you see that you can want things without knowing that you want them, that you can feel things without knowing that you feel them, and that you can *be* things without knowing that *you are them.*

But deeper than the personal unconscious, there is what Jung calls the collective unconscious; a universal layer of the psyche beyond the life and experience of "you".

"The collective unconscious comprises in itself the psychic life of our ancestors' right back to the earliest beginnings. It is continually striving to lead all conscious processes back into the old paths." – Carl Jung

Jung posited the existence of this deep psychic substratum underlying human consciousness after his readings into the myths of various religions as well as his discussions with patients suffering from psychosis. In both cases, Jung observed uncanny similarities in the structure and content of the stories (in the case of the world religions) and delusions (in the case of his psychotic patients) that pointed to a force in the psyche beyond the purely personal.

The collective unconscious is ancient and has been inherited from our ancestors. It is instinctual, and yet it is more than mere instinct due to mankind's recent evolutionary acquisitions of self-reflexive consciousness and imaginative thought.

The mechanism by which the collective unconscious influences the conscious personality is the archetype. It is this idea of the archetype that gives explanation as to why God and transcendence are as central to the human experience as food and sex. God is an objective force in the psyche; a deep reality in the life of the individual and society.

"We can also find in the unconscious qualities that are not individually acquired but are inherited, e.g. instincts as impulses to carry out actions from necessity, without conscious motivation. In this deeper stratum, we find archetypes. These instincts and archetypes together form the collective unconscious." - Carl Jung

The Jungian idea of archetypes (the contents of the collective unconscious) arises in part from the instinctual intelligence of nature. Archetypes are patterns of unconscious representation that result from eons of social and physical interaction between an organism and its environment.

Archetypes lure the fantasy dream currents of the creative unconscious down pre-formed channels.

"Archetypes resemble the beds of rivers: dried up because the water has deserted them, though it may return at any time. An archetype is something like an old watercourse along which the water of life flowed for a time, digging a deep channel for itself. The longer it flowed the deeper the channel, and the more likely it is that sooner or later the water will return." – Carl Jung

For eons of evolution, humans have faced similar challenges and life events. These events, when mixed with the human capacity for thematic abstraction and creative imagination, give rise to *archetypal motifs*, which spring up from man's attempt to explain this universe through creation myths or "end time" prophecies, or *archetypal events*, such as birth, romantic love, and death. All such happenings are given ritualistic significance because they have been burned into our instinctual and behavioral psyche after eons of generational repetition.

The unconscious power of the archetype is largely ignored in modern culture, and so these forces operate within the hidden depths of our psyche, forcing us to act in ways that we do not consciously intend, making us feel emotions that we do not understand, that arise for no apparent reason, and pushing our futures down life paths that we have not chosen.

As Jung states, the great man's calling is never chosen by him alone. It is mandated by powers beyond him, and what makes him great is his willingness act out his vocation and fulfill the law of his being no matter the consequences. In my case, this law, this calling, was born through that spiritual vision, due to my merging with a Force beyond myself in timeless bliss.

This vision, which is more like a living reality in the collective unconscious, is the vision of the

Self. This Self is the central archetype of the psyche according to Jung. These archetypes are instinctual and spiritual intelligences manifesting as *patterns of behavior* when it comes to our relationship to the environment and as *primordial images* and symbols when it comes to our relationship to the unconscious within.

Jung writes, "Thus a word or an image is symbolic when it implies something more than its obvious and immediate meaning. It has wider "unconscious" aspect that is never precisely defined or fully explained. Nor can one hope to define or explain it. As the mind explores the symbol, it is led to ideas that lie beyond the grasp of reason."

These primordial images are visual representations of reality burned into our unconscious. The creative intelligence of mother nature is also within human nature. Our dream and visionary psyche, the creative power of the instinctual unconscious, has been given *symbolic* form over eons of humans facing similar life events and living in a universe built upon opposites and the relationship between these opposites.

Let me put it simply. We have the reality of the universe inside of us. Our primitive ancestors experienced and understood the deepest, most profound, and simple truth of existence: the paradoxical nature of things, or the reality and relationship of opposites. This truth, which most people do not experience directly because most people interact with the collective unconscious through egoic filters, is represented in various fashion throughout the world; as the Taoist yin-yang symbol, the Christian cross, and the images of mandalas (the Sanskrit word for circle) and bindus (the Sanskrit word for center) found in most cultures around the world.

"The mandala symbolizes, by its central point, the ultimate unity of all archetypes." – Carl Jung

The Self is the center and circumference of the psyche. This is the Reality that entered my life on that fateful day smoking hash. The Self is a force beyond the separate sense of self called the ego. This Self is God. It is the highest realization of one's life. It is a withdrawal of the projective tendency of humans to place divinity beyond and outside of themselves.

But we must be very careful here, since this realization of the Self within oneself, the process of individuation, can easily be hijacked by our baser impulses to status and power leading to cult leader-like ego inflation. The ego is not the Self. Your little body and mind are not the Self. Everything is the Self and you are everything. This truth, this unity consciousness, shows you that your deepest nature is something ineffable and transcendent; beyond any graspable reality.

"It is, in fact, impossible to demonstrate God's reality to oneself except by using images which have arisen spontaneously or are sanctified by tradition, and whose psychic nature and effects the naïve-minded person has never separated from their unknowable metaphysical background. He instantly equates the effective image with the transcendental x to which it points." - Carl Jung

During my blissful experience of the Self, I was taken beyond the archetypal symbol. What began as an image was left behind as I merged into a transcendental Reality that ended in the complete loss of consciousness. So what began as an image gave way to that metaphysical unitive background of existence that Jung speaks of; what the Hindus call Satchitananda (being-consciousness-bliss). The experience was so powerful that it destroyed the one who experiences. The little me was drowned in an ocean of indescribable oblivion.

"As a totality, the Self is a *coincidentia oppositorum*, it is therefore bright and dark and yet neither." - Carl Jung

I did not know it at the time, but this transpersonal experience initiated my spiritual journey and activated the individuation process within my psyche. Slowly, I began the process of inner transformation, shifting the center of my psyche from ego to Self. The problem is that this inward journey usually takes place in the second half of one's life; long after the ego has established itself in the world. In my case, the Self emerged long before I knew who I was, even on the level of ego. This is one reason my spiritual journey was so painful, as you shall soon see.

"The Self is thus the supreme psychic authority and subordinates the ego to it. The Self is most simply described as the inner empirical deity and is identical with the imago Dei (God-image). Jung has demonstrated that the Self has a characteristic phenomenology. It is expressed by certain typical symbolic images called mandalas. All images that emphasize a circle with a center and usually with the additional feature of a square, a cross, or some other representation of quaternity, fall into this category.... There are also a number of other associated themes and images that refer to the Self. Such themes as wholeness, totality, the union of opposites, the central generative point, the world navel, the axis of the universe, the creative point where God and man meet, the point where transpersonal energies flow into personal life, eternity as opposed to temporal flux, incorruptibility, the inorganic united paradoxically with the organic, protective structures bringing order out of chaos, the transformation of energy, the elixir of life – all refer to the Self, the central source of life energy, the fountain of our being which is most simply described as God." –Edward Edinger, Jungian Analyst

Chapter 4

Everything changed after that initial spiritual experience. For the next year or so, I felt strange and separate from the world. A feeling of unreality had seized my soul. I cut myself off from social relationships. I was awkward and unsure of myself. I dove into spiritual practice and devoured holy texts from the world religions.

I did not know it at the time, but the individuation process had begun. There are many qualities to this process, but let me simplify and summarize. Individuation is...

(1) "a process in which the ego becomes increasingly aware of its origin from and dependence upon the archetypal psyche."
 - Edward Edinger

(2) a "centralizing process or the production of a new center of personality." - Carl Jung

(3) the transformation of the individual to become all that he is destined to be; the fulfillment of his unique potential.

(4) bringing to awareness various archetypal forces within oneself; the process of integrating these forces; weaving the conscious and unconscious psyche together.

This process of finding the true Self and realizing my unique calling took the shape of Hindu philosophy and meditation. Over and over, I picked up hints that my blissful experience was not insubstantial, that it wasn't some ephemeral illusion, but something real and lasting. The Bhagavad Gita, the foundational text of Hinduism, describes my experience succinctly.

"His mind is dead

To the touch of the external:

It is alive

To the bliss of the Atman.

Because his heart knows Brahman

His happiness is forever."

And yet, despite knowing that the experience was real, my approach to integrating it was one sided. For whatever reason (drug use), the blissful archetype had created a separation in my psyche. I had not realized the Self. I had just gotten a taste of it.

As a child of both the east and the west, I needed both eastern and western psychological frameworks to integrate the lived reality that had now entered my life, and yet I was unable to connect the dots and I did not really understand the experience. I was confused and disoriented. I vaguely put together the bliss that the Gita discussed and my own experience, but for some reason, I could not see any more than that.

Nevertheless, even though my conscious mind did not know, the process of individuation was taking place underneath the surface. And yet, due to my drug use, the more that I meditated, the more disconnected I was from the unconscious parts of myself and the world outside. The fault lines within and without grew deeper. The feeling of separation and unreality became more intense over time.

My spiritual practice became a monster with a life of its own. I meditated hours a day. I tried to purify and restrict my sexual appetites, repressing the unconscious instincts instead of integrating them. I had no guidance and was delving into ever deeper spiritual waters without knowing the danger.

The individuation process, in order to succeed, requires a balancing of the many elements of the psyche. Wholeness is its goal. The acorn is meant to become the oak tree, but my practice deformed and maimed this process while simultaneously speeding it up. Normally, a graceful shift into Selfhood involves the harmonious integration of the following forces or archetypes within the individual:

(1) Persona – "the persona is a complicated system of relations between consciousness and society, fittingly enough a kind of mask, designed on the one hand to make a definite impression upon others, and, on the other hand, to conceal the true nature of the individual." - Carl Jung

(2) Shadow – define later

(3) Anima/Animus – define later

(4) The Self -

"Until you make the unconscious conscious, it will direct your life and you will call it fate." - Carl Jung

The essential quality of the process of individuation is paradoxical in a sense. It requires that we break away from the narratives and influences of society, thereby becoming a more authentic version of our individual nature, as well as become conscious of the unconscious within us, thereby giving us greater understanding of and therefore freedom from the ancient forces within that greatly influence the conscious mind. In this sense, individuation is the process of regaining our autonomy and freedom to choose the kind of life that we want to live.

And yet, paradoxically, the individuation process is also a spiritual journey, aligning the self with transcendent inner realities and the outer currents of the universe. To individuate means to become all that one can be; it means to break down the barriers between the individual and nature, the individual and society, and the individual and herself. So in a sense, becoming a source of good for the collective, a productive member of society, requires that we surrender ourselves to a process within and without that is much bigger than ourselves. To align with the inner Self is to align with God, the union of opposites, and thereby find harmony within and without.

And yet, as I mentioned, for me this process was out of whack from the beginning. A spiritual awakening had created a separation in my psyche, and this next section (recognizing the persona) will illustrate the way in which this feeling of separation manifested itself.

Stage 1

The Persona

"The aim of the individuation process is nothing less than to divest the self of the false wrappings of the persona on the one hand, and of the suggestive power of primordial images on the other." - Carl Jung

As mentioned, the persona is a social mask that one wears in his interactions with others in order to make a definite, usually positive, impression while also hiding his true nature. It is natural and right to have some kind of persona, as human society requires smooth goal oriented interactions for the good of the whole. Nevertheless, the persona becomes maladaptive when the individual becomes over-identified with it. That is, they forget that they are wearing a mask and never take it off. Appearance takes the place of reality.

Such identification emerges from an ego that is excessively tied to social realities such as status, power, money, reputation and image, and this creates an inauthentic personality that consequently causes a subtle separation in one's psyche. Individuality is repressed in the interests of social conformity. The persona is an archetype of the collective unconscious since much of its makeup arises from eons of evolutionary interaction. It becomes harmful when it becomes inauthentic, and it becomes inauthentic when the individual turns into a mouthpiece for the conventions and narratives of society; when the person has no unique and reflective thought of her own.

"[The persona] is, as its name implies, only a mask of the collective psyche, a mask that feigns individuality, making others and oneself believe that one is individual, whereas one is simply acting a role through which the collective psyche speaks." - Carl Jung

The individuation process begins when one clearly sees that they do in fact have a persona. Sometimes, a sudden spiritual awakening strips away the persona, as in my case. Sometimes, the individual consciously initiates the individuation process, as they begin to investigate the unconscious layers within. In both cases, the process (eventually) results in a deep realization on the part of the individual; that they are much more than the conscious mind and persona; that they are, in a very real sense, a paradox; an entity straddling both sides of duality; good and evil; conscious and unconscious.

"The convictions one has about oneself are the most subtle form of persona." - Carl Jung

Nevertheless, this deep realization was not immediately apparent to my immature mind. In my case, the persona was obliterated in an instant. Indeed, this social mask was stripped away long before the development of any healthy ego or stable sense of self. I remember in college that I always did things simply because I was expected to do them. I remember the first week, realizing how much freedom I had and how I could become anyone that I wanted to be; a fresh slate. Immediately, I fell into the role of party boy. I did things that I never chose to do, and said things that I didn't really believe.

Yet my experience of God and timeless bliss blew my "party boy" identity to pieces. In a matter of weeks, I gave up drugs. I told my parents the truth about my failing grades. I broke off contact with most of my friends. I started reading the Bhagavad Gita. I switched my college major to philosophy, political science, and economics. And these external changes mirrored an internal shift in consciousness.

It is hard to explain, but after the spiritual experience, my experience of reality changed. I found something transcendent and lost it again, but the encounter with the Self left something of its mark upon me. The world both felt more real and strange at the same time. I dove into spiritual books like Ken Wilber's Sex, Ecology, and Spirituality and Eckhart Tolle's A New Earth. I had moments of unity consciousness during this time, but more often than not I felt isolated, confused, and alienated.

"one result of the dissolution of the persona is the release of fantasy...disorientation." - Carl Jung

An inner separation had occurred that I could not heal because I didn't know it existed. More than anything, I did not truly understand the depth and the significance of the process that the experience of the Self had initiated in my consciousness. The central archetype of the collective unconscious had made itself known to my conscious ego, and yet just as quickly, it had retreated back into the shadowy depths. And yet the barrier had been crossed. Some boundary within my psyche was broken, and the unconscious power of the Self-archetype was now influencing the direction of my life.

Alongside the death of my persona, the eruption of the Self archetype (the God-image) into my waking consciousness had two behavioral effects: (1) I became socially awkward and weird. (2) I became obsessed with spirituality. These two things ultimately deformed my individuation process.

The spiritual experience had opened many doors within the corridors of my psyche. Archetypes, once dormant, were now awakened and infused by the living waters of my primordial self. As mentioned, the deepest archetype is the Self, but closely tied to this reality are other archetypal realities, like the divine child, the hero, the savior, the Mother, and the Old Wise Man. Ideally, these dream archetypes help the individual navigate the next phase of the individuation process: dealing with the Shadow.

Stage 2

The Shadow

Unfortunately, this is where everything in my story goes tits up. Instead of integrating the shadow, I repressed the dark side. The shadow has both personal and collective qualities to it. On a personal level, socialization often pushes the shadow elements out of a person's conscious identity, resulting in disowned energies and unrealized truths about one's nature. On a collective level, the shadow plays out in the sphere of culture and politics, creating polarization and division due to the individual's tendency to ignore the shadow within herself, and yet without hesitation project this shadow onto others while simultaneously condemning the other as demonic and evil.

As mentioned, the shadow houses all of the darker elements of an individual's personality; those asocial tendencies more or less present in all humans. Yet paradoxically, the process of getting to know these less than desirable parts of oneself heralds a great transformation.

Knowledge of the personal shadow profoundly influences the way you perceive reality. Indeed, it forces the individual into moral development because the confrontation with one's own evil, the loss of any illusion about what you truly are, breaks down belief in simplistic moral and social doctrines and forces the individual to adopt a more contextual and flexible moral framework; one that balances the yin and the yang.

In a deep sense, the individuation process is about reconciling the essential contradiction within us; the existence of good and evil. And yet, this is not what happened in my case. I did not own up to my dark side. Instead, I ignored it. I repressed it. And the consequences were nothing short of total madness: ego inflation and psychotic delusion.

"When one tries desperately to be good and wonderful and perfect, then all the more the shadow develops a definite will to be black and evil and destructive....The fact is that if one tries beyond one's capacity to be perfect, the shadow descends into hell and becomes the devil." - Carl Jung

After the spiritual experience, all of my "bad boy" character traits went underground. I conveniently forgot my past; about all of the drug use and pornography. My personality also transformed (or so I thought) within the space of days. I jumped into personal development. I read books about God, meditated to world peace and loving-kindness chants, and ate only vegan food (because animals have feelings too); all the while completely unaware that my disowned shadow was growing darker and darker.

This pattern continued for about one year. All the while my personality got weirder and weirder. I would avoid people. Sometimes, I walked around campus with a cellphone to my ear, pretending to talk to someone when in truth no one was on the other end. The temporary dissolution of my ego destroyed my persona. I felt that the world was false because, in a deep sense, I was false. Instead of accepting the fact that I am a complex creature with many drives and contradictory tendencies, I desperately clung to all that was holy within me, while ignoring all that was unholy.

"By not being aware of having a shadow, you declare a part of your personality to be non-existent." – Carl Jung

And yet, something inside of me sensed that things were off. Every day in college, I would draw the yin-yang symbol over and over and over again in my notebook. At the time, the act was completely spontaneous. I didn't know why I was doing it, and I didn't look into it too deeply. Only later would I discover that Carl Jung went through this same phase. Throughout his life and during his explorations into the unconscious, Jung created dozens of beautiful mandalas. Unlike me, Jung quickly realized that this spontaneous action had deeper meaning.

"In such cases it is easy to see how the severe pattern imposed by a circular image of this kind compensates the disorder of the psychic state – namely through the construction of a central point to which everything is related, or by a concentric arrangement of the disordered multiplicity and of contradictory and irreconcilable elements. This is evidently an attempt at self-healing on the part of Nature, which does not spring from conscious reflection by from an instinctive impulse." – Carl Jung

"The mandala is an archetypal image whose occurrence is attested throughout the ages. It signifies the wholeness of the Self. This circular image represents the wholeness of the psychic ground or, to put it in mythic terms, the divinity incarnate in man." – Carl Jung

Looking back on it, this was the psyche trying to come back into balance. It was the Self trying to make itself known to the conscious ego. And yet even this desperate attempt at psychological balance was doomed to failure. The blissful experience of the Self had temporarily connected the conscious, unconscious, and collective unconscious within me. It had temporarily made everything one in Consciousness. But paradoxically, this oneness created a schism in my psyche. The mandala drawing was a band-aid, and the pressure of the unconscious continued to build inside of me. The unreality and illusion grew more powerful as the desire for Reality and Truth built up within the transcendent unconscious. Eventually, the universe arranged itself in such a way that a friend offered me two sugar cubes of powerful LSD.

"Although I have never taken the drug [mescalin] myself nor given it to another individual, I have at least devoted 40 years of my life to the study of that psychic sphere which is disclosed by the said drug: that is the sphere of numinous experiences." - Carl Jung

The night that I took the psychedelic was the most profound, mind-blowing night of my life. I took it right before entering a movie theater where I watched, Red Tails; a movie about the Tuskegee Airmen; the first group of African American fighter pilots during World War II. The movie itself is pure action, but with deep thematic undertones of the black man's struggle against discrimination and structural inequality.

As the LSD took hold, the movie itself became a meditative experience for me. I entered this transcendent state of oneness where I literally became the black men in that movie. I felt so deeply their desires and their suffering. It was such a profound experience of empathy that it is impossible to put into words.

Later, as I made my way home, the LSD experience only grew wilder. The roads bent and twirled like bowls of spaghetti. Once I got home, I watched the flowers on my pillows dance and bounce up and down. Another painting of a tree came to life as the leaves waved hello. These sensual experiences were fun, but things got really deep later that night. In what can only be called the deepest and most self transcendent realization of pure Being that I have ever experienced, I fell into this state of complete unity consciousness. Anshu ceased to exist. Everything became God, the pure Self. The experience is impossible to put into words, and long before I knew who Ramana Maharshi was, I spontaneously started the practice of Self-inquiry. For the next I don't know how long but it must have been hours, I asked over and over, "Who am I?"

And the answer that Reality kept showing me was so beyond comprehension that I simply had to ask the question ("Who am I?") again. I looked into myself and found that I didn't exist. The reality of Anshu had turned into the Reality of the All.

This experience of the Self has been pointed to by the ancient sages of India. Jung apparently decided to call his central archetype the Self in light of the Indian philosophical notion of Brahman, or the Nondual Reality, being at the core of man's own divinity. This divinity manifested within me (and I'm hypothesizing here) as the duality between my little self and the archetype of the Self disappeared. The collective unconscious was made fully conscious in the Reality of the Self.

Normally, archetypes are integrated in the individuation process as elucidated by Jung, but this integration is not union. It still has duality tied to it. There is still some barrier between the unconscious instinctual energy of the archetype and the transcendent stillness of pure consciousness itself.

Meanwhile, union requires the complete dissolution of the ego; the complete boundlessness of the Self; the complete merging of the Light of consciousness with the dark of the collective unconscious. This is enlightenment; a realization through which all barriers dissolve.

Chapter 5

Detour into Indian Spirituality

"The hero's main feat is to overcome the monster of darkness: it is the long-hoped-for and expected triumph of consciousness over the unconscious."
– Carl Jung

In the end, the ego can never achieve the final victory of light over darkness, of love over hate, of cosmic consciousness over the collective unconscious. Why? Because the ego exists as a boundary; a division between the conscious and unconscious. The showdown between light and dark can never truly happen so long as the light, in the desperate attempt to maintain its integrity, refuses to enter the dark. Paradoxically, this refusal is maintained by the idea that the light must fight against the dark. The fight comes from duality, from separation, from fear. And yet the fight is necessary. The integrity of the light must exist to, paradoxically, give itself over in sacrificial love to the dark. This sacrifice, this submersion of the undying light to the dark, again paradoxically, results in the spiritual victory of light over darkness.

The life of Jesus is a story of this process. And yet, for whatever reason (the ego enhancing qualities of western civilization perhaps), the Westerns religions have refused to give up the fight, to resist no more. The west's moral and spiritual growth has been stunted by the burden of ego consciousness. The realization of the unconditional love of Jesus, the pinnacle of moral attainment, escapes most people in Western Christendom due to the dualistic power of ego consciousness; a consciousness instinctually tied to the body and the mind.

For this reason, the west must turn east to revivify its religious traditions, to give intellectual rigor to its highest moral ideals through eastern paradoxical thinking, and to give spiritual energy to its deadened rituals and symbols through eastern meditative practices that tap into deep wellsprings within the personal and collective unconscious. Jung explains:

"The clearest expression of this is the Christian reformation of the Jewish concept of the Deity: the morally ambiguous Yahweh became an exclusively good God, while everything evil was united with the devil. It seems as if the development of the feeling function in Western man forced a choice on him which led to the moral splitting of the divinity into two halves. In the East the predominantly intuitive intellectual attitude left no room for feeling values, and the gods – Kali is a case in point – could retain their original paradoxical morality undisturbed." – Carl Jung

In the western traditions, evil is not only split off from the good, but the good itself is pushed onto an otherworldly Father in heaven; a result of a highly developed but still dualistic ego consciousness. Such splitting has caused no small amount of suffering in the history of western civilization. As mentioned, the repression of darkness only makes it more terrible and insidious. The collective shadow, repressed in part by the Christian tradition, has manifested in terrible ways (e.g. Nazi Germany) due to Western man's inability to integrate the darkness with the light. The inability to see one's own shadow, and the unconscious desire to project that shadow onto some metaphysical other (the devil) or an actual other (the Jews in the case of the Nazis), is the necessary consequence of the mind and culture created split between man's conscious ego and unconscious instincts.

Meanwhile in India, the mystical strain of ego dissolution is much stronger; baked as it is into the very fabric of Indian culture and religion. The Indian yogi consciously works with the unconscious, using meditation and yoga to enter and sometimes completely erase the chaotic instinctual multitude of the personal and perhaps even collective unconscious. This process, of maintaining detached conscious awareness while simultaneously releasing the unconscious controlling mechanism of the ego, allows the yogi to fall into the dream world of the unconscious while maintaining poised wakefulness. The yogi does not seek to escape the wonder and horror of his dual and paradoxical nature. Instead, he dives into himself, exploring the depths and heights until he finds that, ultimately, he does not exist; that he is nothing, and in that nothing, he is everything. He becomes God.

"The West is always seeking to uplift, but the East seeks a sinking or deepening....The European seeks to raise himself above this world, while the Indian likes to turn back into the maternal depths of Nature." - Carl Jung

If this practice is aligned with other things, such as bhakti yoga (devotional love of God), karma yoga (selfless service to humanity), and jnana yoga (intellectual inquiry into Truth), then the yogi becomes a fully functioning human being, living a life of purpose and bliss as they engage the world with their entire body, mind, and spirit. This practice shifts the paradoxical, grayish, and seemingly morally relative focus of Indian ethics (a necessary step in the cultivation of unconditional love) into complete union; a process of healing the psyche that gets one in touch with the bliss at the basis of creation.

"The Goal of Eastern practices is the same as that of Western mysticism: the focus is shifted from the "I" to the Self, from man to God. This means that the "I" disappears in the Self, and the man in God." - Carl Jung

This experience, the union of the conscious and unconscious within the Self, is the spiritual equivalent of two lovers in sexual union with each other. Such an existence is the highest end of human being. It is Truth, Knowledge, and Bliss. It weakens and integrates the darkness of the shadow into the Light; and this is done by creating a spiritual culture beyond judgment and ego; one of unconditional love that embraces the light and darkness within all humans.

"In India I was principally concerned with the question of the psychological nature of evil. I had been very much impressed by the way this problem is integrated in Indian spiritual life...by the fact that these people are able to integrate so-called "evil" without "losing face." - Carl Jung

But we must be careful. Let us not become too one sided in our love of nonduality, integration, and oneness. We must work with duality, discernment, and the active separation of our holy qualities from our bestial nature. Having a healthy ego is awesome. Having a charismatic and loving persona is great. But these secondary psychological realities must be transparent and humble within the Light of God. They must shine with divine ecstasy. They must be used in service of a higher good.

"Everything requires for its existence its own opposite, or else it fades into nothingness. The ego needs the Self and vice versa." - Carl Jung

The emphasis of ego boundaries and duality is particularly important in the west for social reasons. Drugs run rampant in America today. The American psyche is not as pure as the Indian. Most American youth who get into eastern spirituality have already been blindsided by the sexual degradation, violent media, and drug fueled mania of American culture. We cannot obliterate the unconscious instincts like the Indian can. Why? Because we are conditioned to immerse ourselves in mindless hedonism from early adolescence.

This is why my LSD trip, while amazing, ultimately had catastrophic results for the functioning of my psyche. I was thrown into the deepest dimensions of cosmic consciousness; the realization of the Self. And yet this attempt to swallow the collective unconscious, archetypes and all, was doomed to failure because the state of Selfhood was not lasting. It was transient and ephemeral. Like any drug, psychedelics pick you up and put you right back down.

Later that night, after the Self-realization experience had ended, I was possessed to go masturbate to porn for some God-only-knows reason, and then I went to sleep while still experiencing the effects of the acid. That night, my dreams were the craziest of my life. But it wasn't the dreams that made it crazy. It was the fact that I was completely awake while sleeping at the same time. It was the strangest state of consciousness. I slept while awake for hours until the acid trip finally ended in the wee hours of the morning.

Chapter 6

Divine Madness

"There is the possibility that a drug opening the door to the unconscious could also release a latent, potential psychosis." – Carl Jung

The next few weeks after the LSD were some of the most harrowing of my life. I don't remember exactly what happened, but this is the synopsis: For a few days, I was disoriented but my ego structure had not broken down yet. Everything felt strange like a dream, but the psychotic unconscious only took over after a few days.

It started with the voices. I was taken over by them. I started talking to otherworldly beings in my head, driving around Atlanta completely out of my mind. A few times, these beings told me to swerve in traffic, which led to a couple of dangerous incidents and my car tire popping. I was stranded on the side of the road in the middle of the night; where I proceeded to wander the fields thinking that I was God. I began punishing all of the evil people in the world with my godly powers. I actually thought that they were suffering just from the divine power of my intentions. I punished all of the wicked, and especially those that caused me harm in the past.

"In introjection, he gets involved in a ridiculous self-deification, or else a moral self-laceration. The mistake he makes in both cases comes from attributing to a person the contents of the collective unconscious. In this way he makes himself or his partner either god or devil." - Carl Jung

Somehow, my parents picked me up, but the voices didn't stop. Even as I write these words today, I feel incredible guilt in my heart. I put my parents through so much. They took out the handles to the doors because I locked myself in my room, talking to imaginary people. I got into a couple of fights with my dad. Eventually, they could not put up with me any longer and sent me to a troubled men's home in Maine.

So here we will pause the story and examine the nature of my psychotic break. First, prior to any psychedelic drug use, I had an experience of blissful oneness and an archetypal vision of the Self. Second, in line with the Jungian idea that the Self is divinity manifested in the mind, once this force in the collective unconscious was released during the psychedelic experience (which causes the temporary dissolution of the boundary between ego and unconscious), my mind fell into religious delusionary fantasies as my ego brought the Self down and identified the oneness of Truth with the separateness of my body-mind. The unitive Godhead did not become Anshu, which is Truth. Instead, little Anshu became God, which is a lie and psychotic fantasy.

"the dark side of the Self is the most dangerous thing of all, precisely because the Self is the greatest power in the psyche. It can cause people to 'spin' into megalomania or fall into other delusionary fantasies that catch them up." - Marie-Louise Von Franz, Jungian Analyst

The dark side of the Self, the archetype of wholeness and the union of opposites, was fractured and brought down into unholy separation and ego inflation due to the fact that the collective unconscious (an ocean of manifold energy and ancestral power) swallowed my little teacup ego, drowning the little me within its depths and hypnotic sway. Bringing the Indian perspective into this, the 'dark side' of the Self only has power so long as the Light of God is not completely integrated into the psyche; the dark side only has power so long as the ego has not been transcended; so long as the separate self has not been consumed by one's union with the true Self; the blissful loving boundless unitive source of existence.

And thus, I lost my mind. I had only temporarily realized the Self. My ego soon reasserted itself alongside a newly punctured hole and permeable boundary between my conscious and unconscious self.

"[Schizophrenia] lowers the threshold of consciousness, thereby allowing normally inhibited contents of the unconscious to enter consciousness in the form of autonomous invasions." – Carl Jung

And yet, and I'm hypothesizing here, because I had previously realized the blissful Self-archetype prior to my acid induced psychotic break, a healing power, a deeper Truth within my psyche beyond the ego, was already working to straighten me out. Now that the unconscious had released and inflated my conscious ego, the unreality that I felt in the months leading up to the LSD experience had now taken over. My psyche was trying to keep this unreality and illusion at bay. The acid blew the whole thing apart. And you know what they say: Often, the only way out is through. This was the case for me. In the few months in Maine, my psychosis became more manageable as the Self slowly disentangled itself from my ego.

The delusions evolved into something a little more realistic (only a little). I no longer talked to the voices in my head while other people were around. I was able to interact somewhat normally. Nevertheless, when I was alone, the delusions and psychotic fantasies always took over again.

"Here we see the characteristic effect of the archetype: it seizes hold of the psyche with a kind of primeval force and compels it to transgress the bounds of humanity. It causes exaggeration, a puffed-up attitude (inflation), loss of free will, delusion, and enthusiasm in good and evil alike."
– Carl Jung

Specifically, the savior archetype replaced the Self-archetype as the thing that my ego identified with. I no longer believed that I was God. The delusions shifted. I was now the savior of the human race; the next Jesus Christ or Buddha; the highest souls in the hierarchy of souls in the world. I had thirty wives. I had conversations with the most famous saints, philosophers, and musicians in history. I talked to Thoreau, the Beatles, some Sufi mystics, Dave Matthews, Eckhart Tolle and many other folks that I cannot recall.

I spent about three months in Maine. During that time, I experienced some of the most profound states of unity consciousness, particularly in nature. Bonneville is one of the quaintest cute cities by the ocean that you will ever find. The nature there is absolutely stunning. During fall, the trees are explosions of color and the forest trails are beds of red-gold fire. The mountains are white and the lakes are the clearest blue. The creative brilliance of nature set my own creative drive alight. Poems of adoration to nature bloomed from my pen. These experiences were some of the most pristine and clear headed moments of my time in la-la land. For a brief moment here and there, I was normal. I was still. I was beyond thought in the timeless now.

But always, the delusions quickly took back over. I fell deeper into the madness as time went on. I believed that dozens of wives were waiting for me beyond some spiritual veil. Finally, one day, the insanity came to a crescendo. My imaginary wives told me to run away from the troubled men's home. They said we are just around the corner. One day, I simply walked out the door and went on a twenty mile hike; unable to find the women that loved me so much. I starved for a couple of nights. I slept cold under the stars. Looking back on it, I am amazed. It was pure madness. And yet, some good came out of it. My delusion bubble popped. I realized that I was out of my mind. And with that realization came the chance to heal; to leave behind my egoic mind and get back to the truth of the Self.

"The second possible mode of reaction is identification with the collective psyche. This would be equivalent to acceptance of the inflation, but now exalted into a system. In other words, one would be the fortunate possessor of the great truth that was only waiting to be discovered, of the eschatological knowledge that means the healing of nations. This attitude does not necessarily signify megalomania in direct form, but megalomania in the milder and more familiar form it takes in the reformer, the prophet, and the martyr." - Carl Jung

Chapter 7

Being Written By God

Once the delusion bubble disappeared, I was able to get back into college. The strangeness and social awkwardness did not go away, however. My spiritual practice went away, and still there was this deep feeling of being out of alignment, of negativity and illusion within me. Looking back on it, I now realize that it was because I was not in alignment with the Self. There was still too much fragmentation within my psyche. Whenever I smoked weed, I felt this terrible darkness.

And the negativity manifested itself in my social relationships. I got into arguments with college professors. I snubbed friendships. Aside from the occasional experience of joyous unity, all I felt was isolation; a feeling arising from the fact that my ego was separated from the Self. The individuation process had derailed. The blissful vision, the manifestation of God's calling in my life, was ignored and forgotten due to my own ignorance. And yet, the power of the Self is so deep and beyond awareness that its Reality worked through me without my knowing it.

I soon graduated college and started work in a bookstore. I lived with my parents, made minimum wage, and more or less lived a life without purpose. And yet miracle upon miracle, two significant events happened to me during this time.

First, I found the Vedanta Center of Atlanta and connected to the blissful spiritual energy of the Indian mystic and saint, Sri Ramakrishna. I still remember the first night that I went to the temple. It was the strangest experience ever. I was seized by this deep awareness, this deep knowing, that if I walked through the doors of this temple, then my life would change forever. I remember driving around the center about ten times before mustering the courage to walk in.

Second, a deep unconscious force blossomed within my soul, pushing me to start writing. Looking back, it is the strangest thing. I wasn't conscious of it at the time. I thought that I was just writing random stuff about God and reality. I didn't realize that I was creating what would eventually turn into my first book, The Paradoxical Light.

Looking at it through the Jungian framework, I now know that it was the collective unconscious, the divine archetype of the Self, using my mind and hands to create this book. This is basically what a "channeled" book is. The new age movement thinks that those who write channeled books have some "woo-woo" direct metaphysical line to God. They do not. It is simply an archetype, a deep instinctual reality and pattern of behavior, doing its work through you. I did not write my first book. It emerged out of me, out of the Self.

"For the individual, knowing God, is the process of recognizing and assimilating the pressured and paradoxical contents of the Self, which come to consciousness- seek incarnation- within the ego."
– Carl Jung

And to provide proof of this fact, I wrote a fairytale (which you are about to read) while in a transcendental state of consciousness. I was not present while the fantasy was being written. After finishing a Paradoxical Light, I wrote it and put it away for several months. For some reason, I didn't realize that it was story about my own spiritual journey and that I was the hero character, Arsen, in the fairytale. It is so strange thinking about it. I wrote a short story about myself but didn't realize it for months. So weird. Only later during my psychotic break in California did I put the dots together: that the dialogue you are about to read at the end of the fairytale, a dialogue between Arsen and the King (think Arjuna and Krishna), was the Self communicating itself to my ego, whispering its eternal paradoxical truths to my befuddled mind.

"The psychotic is under the direct influence of the unconscious." - Carl Jung

The Jungian Analyst, Edward Edinger, speaks of the great literary works of history that exemplify the same process that happened to me. Here are a few.

1. The Bhagavad Gita – The dialogue between the Arjuna (ego) and the Krishna (Self).

2. Book of Acts, the Bible - Paul's (ego) vision of Jesus (Self).

3. The Red Book - Carl Jung's (ego) encounter with Philemon (Self)

4. Thus Spake Zarathustra - Nietzsche's (ego) encounter with Zarathustra (Self).

Of course, I am just a (slightly) humble nobody, so the story you are about to read cannot be compared to such monumental literary works as these. But all of them, including my own fairytale, were written as a result of the ego's encounter with the Greater Personality as Edinger calls it. Now, the question is: what happens when God touches your life? What happens to the individual when he has been subordinated by deep unconscious and superconscious motives beyond him?

Edinger outlines a four stage process:

1. Encounter – This is the meeting between the ego and the Greater Personality. The Self appears in many different forms out of the collective unconscious, presenting its truths through the personal unconscious in a fashion that speaks deeply to the individual and also to the current social issues facing mankind.

2. Wounding – The ego is disoriented from this encounter, and suffers until he consciously integrates the contents of this encounter; until he

lives his soul's calling and the truth of the Self. The wounding also creates isolation and alienation for the divinely touched individual, since the activated archetype is held by him alone, and he has no one to share with, this deep truth and energy within him.

3. Perseverance – In spite of the trials and incredible suffering created by this connection with the divine (in my case it was jail, psychosis, drug addiction, and loneliness), the ego endures and perseveres, all along the way getting hints from the universe as to the meaning of the experience.

4. Revelation – As a result of the encounter, the wounding, and the suffering, the ego comes back from the depths with a treasure, a meaningful life, and a deep truth to share with his brothers and sisters.

As I write these words in Yogaville, I am relieved to say that I have finally reached the fourth and final stage of this process. It took 14 long years to understand and, more importantly, truly integrate my soul's purpose. Up until one year ago, the individuation process was mostly unconscious. Now finally, my ego has mostly surrendered itself to the Self, consciously working with the archetypes in order to help heal this world of its many dualistic schisms.

So without further ado, here is the archetypal story of my own spiritual journey as told through the eyes of our hero, Arsen Achton. Let's follow along as he goes on a perilous journey to find a magical substance called poliin; the only thing that can save his little town from certain destruction by an evil empire.

"He [Friedrich Nietzsche] says about his way of writing that it simply poured out of him, it was an almost autonomous production; with unfailing certainty the words presented themselves, and the whole description gives us the impression of the quite extraordinary condition in which he must have been, a condition of possession where he himself practically no longer existed. It was as if he were possessed by a creative genius that took his brain and produced this work out of absolute necessity and in a most inevitable way." - Carl Jung

(Note: The first chapter is the longest. The second chapter is the most romantic and beautiful, while the third is the most awesome and spiritually inspired.)

Journey of the Soul

Allegory of Spiritual Awakening

allegory (noun) - a story, poem, or picture that can be interpreted to reveal a hidden meaning, typically a political or moral one.

Chapter 1

Arsen looked up into the cloudy mists high above him. White vapors hit the summit of Mt. Helias. Frequently, those vapors descended into the highlands, making his search for the staircase impossible. He dare not walk too far while these mists swirled about him. One wrong step could send him tumbling down a gorge....a bloody death indeed....

Thinking on it, Arsen realized that he was in a terrible predicament. Food supplies were running low and the damp map in his hands was made eons ago. Perhaps, the mountains had shifted since its making. Many of the marked places were not to be found, though other features were clearly visible. Arsen stood on a large hill, trying to see the mountain through the clouds. He was in the right place....Well, according to the map at least. Yet he still could not make out the silvery blue runes that were carved into the side of Mt. Helias. They were supposed to show the way to the very top.

An owl hooted above him; a sign of the coming night. The wind blew swiftly around his perch, stinging Arsen's fingers as he brought out an old brass telescope. The seeing-eye did nothing to help. The journey had been a failure. If Arsen did not leave soon, his fate would be like that of Aoir. Without food and water, the terrors of the Avirsin wilds were enough to drive even great warriors mad.

Sighing, Arsen climbed down from the mossy boulder. In its shadow, he gathered wood and water to make dinner. He quickly set a fire going and pulled out a small pot, cooking a soft stew of deer meat, honey, salt, and sprigs of herb found on the mountain side. Eating the sparse meal, Arsen looked over the mountain one last time. It stood ominous and regal, like a king too proud to reveal his secrets to passing strangers.

The journey back home would take a few days, and so Arsen decided to get a head start before the evening turned to night. He set off down the steep hills, often slipping and sliding on the wet grasses. The fog soon cleared and, far away, the faint glimmer of the sea could be seen framed by a dying red sun. And upon it, the sight of one hundred war ships met Arsen's eyes. Their red and golden sails swayed as they made for the harbor of Holsi, which had been sealed off and mounted with cannons.

Straining his ears, the faint crack of gunfire could be heard, and every now and then an explosion would light up the darkened skies, sending a ship flaming into the sea. Swallowing heavily, Arsen ran down the hill and off to the edge of the forest. Quite suddenly, a rumble began to build overhead. Arsen looked up to see fat raindrops tumbling through the cypress trees. Lightning flashed in the sky, illuminating dark clouds with a blue glow. An incredibly strong gust of wind caught Arsen in the back, sending him face down into a muddy puddle. Spluttering in amazement, he looked back up the path into the hills. Hurricane force winds tore around Mt. Helias. Arsen could tell by the clouds billowing about the monolith.

A moment's indecision flicked over his face. Going back up the mountain would be a terrible risk. But events in Erisa were moving quickly apace. The Sundrians would break into Holsi within days, and then there would be zero chance of saving his little town. He would have to risk it. Poliin was the only thing with the power to stop the navy currently bearing down upon his home. It was the reason for the Sundrian invasion. The energy in a single drop would bring life to the ancient guardians and cannons of Holsi. Eons ago, the Founder Civilization had flourished in the lands of Avirsi, and their structures still lasted beneath the wooden and stone dwellings of the Holsins.

Arsen climbed back up the mud trail, bending low to the ground and leaning into the wind. The evening sun sent fragments of light over Mt. Helias. Now, the storm winds blew south and the clouds followed like a river. An otherworldly glow faintly emanated from the mountain. Blue-green runes ran along its side, pointing the way into a hidden gorge.

"That must be where the stair starts." muttered Arsen feverishly.

He refused to celebrate just yet. Reaching into his pack, Arsen pulled out a rope and leather belt. He fastened it tightly around his waist. A ridge of stones stood at the edge of the precipice, which fell into a foliage of windswept trees. The descent into the gorge was treacherous and Arsen lost footing several times to be caught painfully by the safe rope. His waist felt bruised and his arms burned from the exertion. After an hour of cold and rain, the jagged rocks turned into the tall grasses of a long valley. The first stars began to turn in the night sky.

Fearfully, Arsen scanned the tree line for wild beasts. Night was the time when mountain lions roamed into the valleys for food. The sunlight was long gone, but Arsen did not make out any gleaming eyes. Small dagger in hand, he walked into the silent wood. A soft, otherworldly glow permeated the evenly spaced trees.

A strange feeling crept over Arsen as he walked. This was no ordinary wood. Nothing seemed to move. No insects stirred. No animals ran above in the canopy or below in the undergrowth. Even the trees appeared frozen, as if the hands of time had never touched them. A young moon shown overhead, but it was not the source of the forest's glow. Walking deeper into the trees, things quickly became stranger.

Arsen blinked several times as a sudden feeling of timelessness took him. For just a moment, he saw a world not belonging to his own, where the moon above was replaced by a blazing sun, and the trees were replaced by a city filled with people. Blearily, he sat down for a moment to gather his wits. What was happening? Arsen prayed he hadn't lost his mind. After resting in the shade of a tall elm, and then, looking to the stars for direction, the young artist stood up and continued eastward.

The otherworldly aura grew stronger as he approached the center of the forest. Ahead, a shining white light cut through the trees so forcefully that Arsen covered his eyes. He crouched low and crept forward with knife in hand, but the light only came from a pathway winding through the trees. Arsen stepped onto the white stone, which led directly towards the mountain. The stones fit perfectly next to each other, as if the walkway had been created earlier that day.

Arsen knelt to touch the trail. "This must be made with incredible ingenuity to last so long," he thought aloud.

Whoever put it there, Arsen was happy for the pathway. With a thrill, he knew his goal lay not five leagues away. The journey went by quickly now, and the mountain grew into a looming monolith.

Arsen reached the base and looked up as the path turned into smooth white stairs. They were carved into the side of the mountain, spiraling around it like a giant serpent. Arsen's jaw dropped as he looked carefully at the blue runes carved along the stairs. They were not runes at all, but incredibly intricate images painted on the side of the mountain. Arsen walked to the images and inspected them one by one. He had never seen artisanship of this quality. It was clear that he had met his match. At some point in time, there existed a painter whose skill surpassed even the greatest known artists of Avirsi.

Each painting changed as he climbed the mountain. They were telling a story. The next day, Arsen climbed the stair quickly. The journey was arduous and his legs burned by mid-morning. Yet Arsen did not slow his rapid ascent. The tale unfolding before his eyes was fascinating. The blue paint on the mountain shone brightly in the morning light.

The pictures told the story of the Founders, starting from the First Era. They spoke of a young man with good heart, who stumbled onto a secret that would change the world forever. Through his alchemy, the boy grew to master incredible powers over nature and time. He used his powers to unite the world under one banner. The power would have corrupted any lesser man. But the boy, now an emperor, never succumbed to the temptation of tyranny. He created a world of peace, justice, and prosperity.

By noon, Arsen had climbed halfway up the mountain. All along the paintings grew grander in scale. Each one now lasted hundreds of feet, detailing the erection of epic civilizations with white cities, golden domes, and wide roads. They showed vast trade routes with city-sized ships sailing from one country to another. The Founders created a world empire. There were pictures of kings shaking hands with other kings. Peace treaties were forged and armies disappeared. None needed fight, for incredible wealth was generated by the power of poliin. No beggars begged. None went hungry, and the First Era became a golden age for the world of Erisa.

All of this Arsen took in with wonder. The past was a perfect time; nothing like the wars and factions of Erisa today. It seemed impossible that this very land, Avirsi, had once been part of a peaceful empire. Sadly, Arsen looked away from the pictures to see how far he had ascended. Light mists of cloud floated by as he looked south towards the sea of Silsilaan. It glittered far away in the sunlight. Squinting, Arsen also made out Holsi. The Sundrians were not yet within the city.

After a brief rest and stale biscuits, Arsen continued upwards. The peak of the mountain was near. Arsen could tell by the tightening spiral of the staircase. Finally, the boy broke through dense white mist onto the flat peak of the mountain. Ahead stood a tall white observatory with a silver dome; out of which poked a gigantic golden telescope. The Founders must have used it to gaze at the stars, figured Arsen. The building did not look a day old, although it must have stood there for thousands of years.

In another time, Arsen would have been giddy with excitement for all of his discoveries. Indeed, he would have used the opportunity to gloat over his professor and peers, leading them to the only known remnants of the Founding Era. But with Sundrian threatening the destruction of all Avirsi, Arsen hurried towards the observatory; his hand resting on the hilt of his dagger.

The setting sun lit a sea of clouds with reds and purples as Arsen walked into the long entrance hall. Brackets with unlit torches graced the walls. Arsen set one alight with flint and checked the many dark rooms of the observatory. They were filled with heaps of scrolls and books. Some were filled with strange golden instruments and telescopes. Arsen looked everywhere for some trace of poliin; finally searching the silver domed main chamber.

The white room was bathed in blue starlight, and above, the dome opened to the actual stars of the night sky. All of this was lost on Arsen, however. His eyes were drawn to the very center of the room; where a well stood carved into the floor. Walking up to the stone well, Arsen looked deep into the darkness, dropping his torch into the center to note the depth. It fell for several seconds before the flame disappeared with a splash. This must be it, he thought. There was no time to waste. Arsen got another torch from the wall and prepared a coil of rope.

He descended into the well slowly, holding the light in one hand. The journey was terribly risky. If Arsen let the rope slip, there would be no way to get back out. A large cavern opened up around him, and underneath ran a smooth river of poliin. Strange sounds issued from the substance flowing swiftly beneath Arsen's torchlight. Under the light, the poliin glowed blue, green, yellow, and other colors Arsen could not make out.

The whispers grew stronger. The sounds seemed lost and timeless, as if they issued from beyond this world. Arsen felt the press of eons upon his thoughts. One whisper came from the distant past, while another came from an unknown future. Intoxicated, the boy leaned closer. He vaguely remembered the warning told by the turbaned potions trader.

"Do not drink of the water, for you will almost surely die. And if you must drink of the water, then do not drink too much or you will surely die."

Arsen had planned on swinging himself to the shore, but those plans changed in an instant. Lowering himself only inches above the river, he held out one finger to touch the poliin. The rope tightened to its limit, groaning as Arsen stretched towards the water. Just as he touched the vapory substance, his snapped with a resounding crack!

Arsen fell head first into the river of poliin, swallowing a mouthful as he struggled for air. His body spasmed and writhed in pain. Desperately, the boy tried to fight the swift current, but could find no purchase in the vapory water. The river flowed inexorably into the deep dark caves of the mountain. Soon, Arsen gave up fighting and let himself be taken. Death would be a calm peace compared to this struggle for life. His lungs filled completely with poliin, and the river carried his body down down down into the darkness. The world slowly disappeared and time lost all meaning.

Chapter 2

After what seemed a year of sleep, Arsen opened his eyes and looked about. Around him lay a neat and tidy bedroom bathed in morning light. Something was strange about the room, however. Indeed, Arsen could sense that something was different about everything around him. Immediately, a flurry of thoughts entered his mind.

"How did survive the fall? I should be dead. Where am I? Whose home am I in?"

The more Arsen wondered, the more scared he became. He needed to get back to his own time. What if the Sundrians had already attacked

Avirsi, destroying his town and only home? Arsen made to get up from the bed, but a blast of pure energy sent him flying back into the covers. Coughing and spluttering, Arsen looked at his hands and feet. They were glowing faintly.

"Don't worry, the poliin surges wear off with time."

Arsen turned toward the doorway to see a young girl; only the girl was not human. Her soft brown eyes were the only part of her body that did not glow gold. Gulping, Arsen tried to stand again.

"What is wrong with my body?" he asked.

"Oh nothing, this happens to every traveler. At least, that's what my grandfather tells me."

Arsen stared at the little girl curiously. "What do you mean traveler? Where am I right now? Or better said: When am I? And how do you know my language? You aren't Avirsin. I know that much."

The girl laughed. "I know your language because it is a descendent of my language. Don't you know that?"

"Oh, yes....and what exactly is your language?" stammered Arsen, dumbfounded.

At that moment, an incredibly old man with golden skin came to the door. His face was wrinkled and squinty, and he wore a flat cap to keep the sun from his eyes. "Hush now, Anya. Leave the poor boy alone. This is Alynia. This is the Center of the Circle."

The old man pointed to a small map on the wall. Upon it was drawn the circle of continents that marked the world Arsen grew up in. In his world, the center of the map was left empty, for no sailor ever survived to speak of whatever lay there. Now, this center was colored in with a large island shaped like a coin.

"Let me introduce myself." said the man, kindly. "I am Honso, the farmer. This is my granddaughter, Anya. It is the First Era; the year 1092. And you are a traveler; one of many who visit us through the mists of time."

Arsen's face began to turn white as the man spoke. "Why am I here? How can I get back to my own time?" he asked, hoarsely.

The old man laughed. "Ah yes...why? It is the universal question. Often, the answer to why is not to be found. But in your case, the answer is very simple. There is soon to be a coronation of the King, and you are invited as his guest of honor."

"Then why am I the guest of honor?" asked Arsen, panicking. He had to get back home. There was no time to waste.

Seeing his face, Honso smiled knowingly. "I know that events in your time are quite....chaotic right at this moment. But do not worry, child. This island is beyond time. We could spend ages here and not move a moment in your world."

"That still doesn't explain why I have to stay here." said Arsen, stubbornly.

"You are free to do what you wish." said Anya. "That is why you are here. To make a choice."

"Hush now, Anya." chided the old man. "You need not weigh his mind with talk of the future. Right now, you should rest and then we can talk. Hopefully by the end of it, I will have convinced you to accompany me to meet our King." The old farmer left Arsen for some minutes and returned with a large tray of cheese, wine, and vegetables.

Over the next few days, Arsen rested and talked with Honso. Poliin still coursed through his veins, and even the deep discussion of the Founders did not stop him from occasionally flying into a tree after an uncontrollable burst of energy.

Mostly, Honso talked while Arsen listened. They talked about this world. They talked much about good and evil, though Honso never spoke in such simple terms. Instead, he would carry on about chaotic orders, heavenly earths, and timeless times.

In a few blinks of the eye, the days turned to years and the years into decades. As the centuries passed, Honso's granddaughter grew from a girl into a young woman and Arsen into a young man. Both of them grew close, deciding to marry and have children. The ages turned like a wheel. The stars came and went. Arsen spent his days working the vineyard to make wine, and milking the cows to make cheese. Other time was spent reading and writing, making love to his wife, and playing with his children.

Arsen learned what it was to exist in God's mind, perceiving infinity in the space of a moment, and also through the vast stretches of real time. Before he knew it, the day of the King's coronation had dawned upon his small valley.

He left his house in the morning half-light in order to water his garden and gather supplies for the journey. Quickly, he walked to a nearby stream of poliin, dumping a bucket into the water and throwing it on the various trees and shrubs of his land. The day before he had planted a cherry tree. Impatiently, he waited as it groaned and creaked under the effects of poliin. One foot. Ten feet. In three minutes, the plant stood fifty feet above his head. Once it stopped growing, Arsen tapped it gently with a walking staff. A shower of red cherries fell from the branches. Holding out a burlap sack, he caught a few hundred for the long journey ahead.

Many people were on the white stone roads by the time Arsen got on his way. Slowly, crowds were making their way along the tree-lined paths towards the capital. Some were playing flutes, walking merrily along. Others had jugs filled with poliin, and were sprinkling plants with water. Trees many hundreds of feet tall stretched still higher. Occasionally, one released a fruit the size of a large clock. Others released leaves and flowers, filling the air with red and gold motion. Arsen fell into step beside Wilas; a farmer who lived over the hill and by the water.

"How goes it, Arsen Achton?!" laughed Wilas, patting him on the back with a large hand.

Arsen lurched forward, smiling ruefully. "You seem mighty excited today."

"Well, it isn't everyday you elect the King back to his throne."

"Yes, but you elect the same king every single eon, over and over." pointed out Arsen. "What is the point of getting excited voting if you don't choose anyone different from time to time?"

"Well....it's because he's a good king." said Wilas, matter of factly. "Doesn't make sense to change what works."

Arsen smiled. It was the simple logic that he had come to expect from Wilas. "So then, who is watching the farm while you're gone?"

"Oh, no one. The gollums will be fine for a few days. I just refilled their energy stores with poliin, and programmed them to carry on the farming without me."

"Oh yes, I forgot about the gollums. I've never used one myself. There is something more fulfilling when you eat the bread of your own labor."

"Oh now, don't judge me too harshly!" laughed Wilas. "I have to feed all of the sages, scientists, and artisans that live within the city, or about ten million people. It is impossible to do so without the help of artificial intelligence."

"And a noble thing you are doing as well." replied Arsen, "For without your labor, the creative wonders of Alscon could never exist."

As they spoke, the capital city came into view; a tall shadow against the evening sky. It stood framed upon a hill, and lines of crowds could be seen filtering into the city from every direction. All were laughing in the half light. The red sun against a purple and golden sky gave the world a dreamy quality.

This was Alscon; the jewel of Alynia. People could be seen walking among the many open air pathways between its golden towers, waiting for the fireworks and feasting that attended the coronation. The air thrummed with magic. Often, the energy of the city would cause it to float into the clouds. If not for the will of a few earthly minded rulers, much of the Founder civilization would fly directly into the heavens.

The rulers maintained the day to day affairs of civilization. They were the Mind of Alynia in a way. Of course, this did not mean that they were a state. Alynia ceased to be a traditional empire centuries ago. The government slowly dissolved as their functions became unnecessary. No one needed protection, for there was no war or violence.

In the years following the Founding, the inhabitants of Alynia had splintered into many communities of varying sizes. Most chose to live in small townships of a few thousand people, organizing their stone houses in large circles. Such a size allowed for a peaceful and simple existence.

Most avoided the city for obvious reasons. In the years following the proliferation of poliin, the Founder race learned that unlimited energy did not create a happy world. The reason for peace was not because of wealth, since wealth often creates greed and malice.

No, the reason for peace was completely subjective. With the abundant magic in Alynia, the absolute union of the child with society was necessary before the child grew a will of his own.

Easily, the power of poliin could spell destruction for the Founders if the wayward will of one person turned evil. Arsen constantly felt the tug towards oneness at the edges of his consciousness. It expanded into stillness as the rulers did their work upon the collective will.

Eventually, as a child moved into adulthood, the borders between self and other gave way to oneness. The individual will died to movements of a greater will, just as a drop of water merges with a flowing river. The Founder world was based upon the coordinated rhythms of the collective will. Of course, this did not mean that the individual wasn't free to act and whatever she pleased. Yet there existed two minds within each Founder. While the free individual operated on the level of thought and action, the collective being operated upon their spiritual consciousness, molding it according to the Form of Good.

Watching the Founders go about their affairs was always a strange sight for Arsen. They moved as if they were One Being, synchronizing perfectly throughout the day. All Founders worked at various occupations. This was not because they needed to. Indeed, this was another thing that the discovery of poliin made apparent. Life became meaningless with too much wealth. Mean became bored and lazy. Idleness dulled the mind and senses. Soon, the King decreed that all must work at an occupation of their choice. Most chose creative occupations like music or art. The city was covered in fantastic paintings and large sculptures. Honors and awards went to those artists who excelled all others. Such cooperative competition served to create a constant stream of inventions for the Founders.

One of those inventions, a small castle, floated over Arsen's head as he entered the golden city. As moving walkways carried him up a steep hill, more of the city came into view. Arranged like a many tiered cake, its golden buildings were covered with green rooftop orchards and winding channels that carried water to small pools.

In these orchards stood people watching the night sky and looking expectantly towards the castle at the top of the hill. Runners distributed pies, tarts, soups, and wine freely to the crowd. A deep peace stole over Arsen during his upwards ascent. At the pinnacle of the city rose the golden domed castle of the King.

Fireworks burst from it to signal the coming crowning. The sheer mass of people made seeing ahead difficult, but the Alynians naturally moved out of the way for Arsen, sensing that his destination had not yet been reached. Past the large courtyards filled with sculptures, and past the famous painting of Alcias (which stretched to two thousand feet), Arsen walked with single minded intensity.

Chapter 3

Reaching the highest room of the castle, Arsen found himself behind a crowd of richly dressed nobles. These were the rulers of Alynia, and they in a semi-circle around the King; the original Founder. He knelt on a dais that looked out onto the masses. Sweet and grand music rose through the city. Slowly, a little child walked up to the King and stood on tip-toe, placing a golden grown on his head. The people broke out in celebration, and the air was filled with smoke and color.

Soon, a scribe stood and read from a long parchment. He droned on about great deeds and noble acts until the King finally interrupted with a polite cough.

"I am sure our fine people have heard enough about me over the eons. Truly, we are not here to celebrate my throne, but to ask one of our own to make a choice."

With this the King turned to Arsen, who walked to the terrace overlooking the city and faraway mountains. The first stars began to shine in the sky. Below, the people had returned to their own nighttime revels.

The King stood before Arsen in fiery robes; tall and golden. "Would you, Arsen, like to know the real story of how I created utopia?" Arsen nodded; his heart racing. "Come, let us sit and talk in private."

The two left the nobles and walked to another marble terrace; filled with small fountains and manicured lawns. At the center stood a small basket tied to spherical balloon. Arsen stepped into the basket, while the King sliced the ropes holding the basket earthbound. Quickly, the balloon drifted upward, over the lights of the city, above the tall forests, to be taken wherever the winds beckoned.

After some time contemplating the rivers below and faraway ocean to the south, the King spoke: "Many in Alynia believe that it is power that created this civilization, but I will tell you the true story of the Founders."

The King settled back into his seat, gathering his thoughts. "When I first found poliin in the ruins of Allendor, I was but a young man. I used its power to gather wealth and friends. Although I never used it for evil purposes, those around me became taken with its power. My brother died in combat. My wife left me. My children were ruined, and all things that once shone with goodness became tainted with corruption."

"In grief, I fled to the forest and disappeared from society. With me disappeared the knowledge of poliin, for I had hidden the source of my power out of caution and greed. For decades, I contemplated the nature of poliin and the ways of the world. I meditated. I wrote, and finally I attained a measure of peace."

Arsen listened to the King's words, gazing thoughtfully out on the rivers below shining in the moon's light. "How then did you create utopia if poliin simply corrupts?"

The King smiled. "I did it very slowly. The power of poliin is such that it attracts those people on a similar frequency to oneself. At first, I used it for selfish reasons, and so the selfish flocked to me. Once I became a hermit, I used it rarely and only then to heal the suffering around me. First, other selfless souls became attracted to me. We created small religious communities, and, over the decades, these holy men and women lost their self-will as the poliin made us One. Soon, our numbers grew into the hundreds and others began to notice our powers. Our lands never had to be tilled. They bore grand harvests year after year. Our children were the most enlightened, intelligent, and kind. We created communities of incredible order and happiness. No crime existed, and no pain ever surfaced."

"Although we began deep in the forests of Scithria, after a point, the news of our power could no longer be hidden. More material souls became attracted to us after seeing our society. These souls took longer to mold, and one selfish youth, in his desire for more, took the news of poliin to a nearby king; proud and cruel."

The King's eyes clouded over as he spoke of the past. "The king attacked us in the dead of night. He razed our lands before our eyes. He kidnapped our children for study, and took our women as his queens."

The King sighed loudly. "I was forced to use poliin to stop his tyranny. I entered his city in blind fury, with hitherto unknown power burning in my veins. Such was my state that I forget my actions, but when I came to, the tyrannical king lay dead at my feet."

"I realized that I could no longer hide from the world around me. There was too much suffering, too much division. I took control of the Sycion, and used my closest advisers to create a peaceful kingdom. I hid the power of poliin from all but those nearest, allowing it to work its wonders over time. Initially, the people believed me to be sorcerer. Some revolted, although soon all saw the benefits of my rule, and the influence of poliin began to permeate the land. Trade began to flower. The people became happy and prosperous. Large cities grew where once stood villages."

"I entered into alliances with the majority of kings. Many good hearted rulers came to me out of love. Others came to me out of prudence. And a few came because of my unrivaled power."

"What did you do with the kings that opposed you?" asked Arsen, "There must have been some."

The King shrugged. "I let them be. I had the majority of rulers on my side, and I knew that given enough time poliin would change the evil ones too."

As they spoke, the balloon drifted beyond the mountains and over the oceans. Below, Arsen heard the call of whales. Their throaty roars reverberated across the starlit waterscape. Many grew to the size of small cities under the influence of poliin, and Arsen saw one monstrous shadow drift beneath them in silence.

The King continued his story; too deep in the past to notice the present. "Eventually, as the centuries passed by, the world reached a critical mass of awakened souls. Wars were fought, but their destruction and suffering only turned more people towards self-transcendence. After a certain point, there took place incredible shifts in culture. We became a spiritualized civilization; completely detached from our warring natures."

The King left off from his story and looked below; where shone a small island with a single light in the center. Slowly letting the helium out of the balloon, the craft drifted on the winds until it landed with a slight thud on the soft grass. The King led Arsen out of the balloon and into the stone ruins of a long forgotten civilization, Allensia.

They walked between the trees, under a gushing waterfall, towards a small pool of poliin glinting under the stars.

"This island is the original source of poliin; the storehouse of a power that bends time and space. And here is where I give you the ultimate choice."

The King turned intently to look at Arsen. "My story is not unique at all. Indeed, it's happening is woven into the very fabric of the universe. Prophets and saints are the sole source of hope for humankind, and it falls upon you to choose whether you are one of them."

Arsen stared, amazed. "So this is the choice all travelers are given? Live here forever with infinite material wealth, or turn back towards your own time, taking with you the wisdom and power that can save the world. But who will listen to me?"

The King reached into the folds of his robes. "Take with you this book. It is the result of eons of study; imbued with magic such that anyone with good heart and mind will feel its power. There are many other kingdoms besides Sundria. Speak to their nobles and kings. You may even change the world without using poliin at all, which is the wisest course for any man."

Arsen thought of his wife and grown up children. He had spent ages by their side. Deep down, he knew he had made up his mind on the matter long before the King even asked. He would leave the City of Heaven for his own earthly home. Arsen smiled to himself. Many people would leave earth for heaven, but not many would go down from heaven to earth, taking with them the knowledge of the King. Only sacrifice and detachment would save Avirsi from Sundria. Only those willing to give up wealth, fame, and immortality can create utopia in any case.

Laughing, Arsen knew that all of this was one huge plan. He was meant to climb Mt. Helias. He was meant to meet to the King. And the King knew that only a spiritual being would give up one side of duality to consciously cross over to the other. With a fond farewell, Arsen stepped into the center pool of water, knowing that his destiny lay in saving the world and creating a brighter future for our children.

"The archetypal image of the wise man, the savior or redeemer, lies buried and dormant in man's unconscious since the dawn of culture; it is awakened whenever the times are out of joint and a human society is committed to a serious error." - Carl Jung

Analysis

The physical geography and chronological events of this story are meant to be understood as the geography and events taking place within my own consciousness. The journey of Arsen symbolizes the individuation process. Arsen is alone in the first chapter; bravely (and desperately) facing the unconscious wilds of Avirsi. If you'll remember, the individuation process naturally creates isolation, since it separates the hero from society and catalyzes the search for greater truth.

Meanwhile, poliin is an infinite power that can save Arsen's little town from an evil empire. The substance represents the archetypal power of the Self. It is the goal. When Arsen falls into the river of poliin, it transports him through time and space into the utopian civilization of the Founders. Similarly, the Self in actuality is beyond time, space, and causation. Submersion in the Self breaks all dualistic barriers and results in the radical transformation of consciousness.

So really quickly, I'm gonna break down the symbolic themes behind the landscape of the first chapter. (This is what the story means for me. It may be different for you.) First, the evil empire stands for the immense power and spiritual corruption of modern culture. The attacked town symbolizes the little guy and the relative weakness of transcendent ideals and selfless morality. The ancient structures upon which the town is built stand for the core of spiritual wisdom within all of the world religions.

The map in Arsen's hands speaks to a deep theme: the disjunction between thought and reality; between the written map and actual territory. If you'll remember, the map was made eons ago and many of the landmarks have changed since its production (speaking to the fact that the truth of past religions must be tailored to the needs of the present day).

The valley speaks to my initial forays into the unconscious. The valley is timeless and Arsen has visions as he walks through it. The valley is nature. The brief vision Arsen has speaks to the intuitive and prophetic power of the unconscious and how it can peer through space and time. The white path in the valley, a path made long ago by the Founders, stands for spiritual wisdom. The ascent up the mountain stands for my growing integration of this moral and spiritual wisdom, and the heightening of my consciousness with spiritual practice.

Also, the story told by the paintings along the mountain speaks to deep a spiritual theme. The boy in the tale is the King. Most significantly, note how the story has a mythical and idealized quality to it, and compare it to the actual tale that the King tells Arsen. The discrepancy between myth and actuality is a major fact in the history of religion. Humans have this tendency to put other humans on a pedestal. Indeed, we have a tendency to put God herself on a pedestal. In both cases, we do this at our peril.

The assumption of the perfection of spiritual leaders has led, consistently, to corruption and suffering. Often in religious cults, followers refuse to question the guru because they assume the guru is all-knowing and all good. They assume the guru is beyond moral standards and critical reproach. Again and again, we find that power corrupts all but the saintliest souls.

This fact is also true when it comes to God. When terrible things happen in our world, we assume that God has done it for reasons we cannot comprehend. First, we assume that God is all powerful like Zeus, and that he can hurl thunderbolts at all of the rapists and serial killers of the world, but he chooses not to because God is beyond moral reproach. This is simply not true.

Also, we assume that there is no dark side to God; that nondual Love is the only divine manifestation, and that dualistic love and hate have nothing to do with the One. Again, this is simply not the case. In the next chapter, we will delve more deeply into the archetype of evil.

But for now, let's return to Arsen. Once he finds the river of poliin beneath the observatory of the Founders, he becomes entranced by its timeless power. The substance overpowers his autonomous will, which represents the power that the Self exercises over the ego. Arsen bends to touch the waters only to have his harness snap and fall in. This event signifies my psychotic break as the collective unconscious overwhelms the conscious ego.

Arsen is transported to the past civilization of the Founders. The Self breaks all barriers of time and space. Similarly in my own life, psychosis changed everything. Time lost all meaning and I no longer identified with my body. Arsen's journey represents the radical shift in consciousness that my psychotic break catalyzed.

And this is where the story begins to shift from being about me and starts to align with the message of my first book.

Very briefly, my first book, the Paradoxical Light: On Utopia vs. Fall of Civilization is about the evolution of humanity, the rise and fall of civilizations, and the potential utopian future of humanity. Arsen wakes up in utopian paradise and the second chapter attempts to paint an image of this ideal future. The world is also symbolic of my inner state of consciousness; the (eventual) bliss and love that I attained once I integrated my initial spiritual experience, my psychotic break, and my life purpose.

And now we get to the final and most important chapter! Here, we have a spiritual dialogue between the ego and the Self. But before we analyze this conversation between Arsen and the King on politics, justice, and corruption, we have to consider perhaps the most important moral statement of this story. In the coronation, the King, the leader of the Founders, kneels before a little child. The most powerful monarch in the world humbles himself before the purity and innocence of a child. It is the child who confers power to the King; not some pope or military leader. It is love that justifies power. Where there is force, there is no love. Where there is love, there is no force.

This theme runs through the story of the King and his creation of utopia as well. Initially, the King finds poliin and uses it to amass power. The use of the archetypal power of the Self for dark motives only creates suffering in the long run. This is what happens to the King, and it exemplifies the story of most every religion. Founders like Jesus and "Krishna" start a religion with high ideals and spiritual motives, but over time this purity diminishes as lesser men use religion to gain wealth and power.

Often, this material corruption pushes true spiritual individuals to the fringes of religion and culture. Mystics and saints leave society for the forests and mountains. And yet sometimes, God inspires some saint to reenter the social fray, using their altruistic morality to gain a following and challenge the existing religious structures of the time. So far in history, this has been the cycle.

1. Moral and spiritual foundation

2. Material corruption over time

3. Reformation and revolution

4. And the cycle begins again.

However, in the story of the King, the cycle is broken. Similarly, in the real world today, the cycle will very likely end in one way or another as humanity accepts some form of world spirituality through the unity of the world religions.

(edinger quote here from his video. How Jung set the foundation for the unity of the world religions and how this unity sets the backdrop for political unity.)

The second half of the King's tale speaks to an idealized version of the story of our current world civilization. The movement of history from science to modernity to industrialization to colonialism to two world wars to our current worldwide economic and political order is discussed in greater detail in The Paradoxical Light, but the story of the King allegorically speaks to this recent history.

Beginning long ago, but picking up steam with the rise of global trade networks, a spiritual philosophy based upon nondualistic oneness begins to grow. You have Indian saints like Swami Vivekananda travelling to America and calling for the unity of the world religions in the 1800's. You have the growing optimism of science and the moral progress of humanity.

Just as the King began his new life in the forest, a new spiritual and moral power starts to rumble within the unconscious depths and conscious heights of the human species. Slowly, this power grows, and yet with greater social popularity comes greater political and economic opportunity. This political and economic opportunity corrupts materialistic souls, leading some to use this new power for selfish gain.

The evil king in the story speaks to both the chaos of World War I and II, and also the moral corruption of both ancient religions and the more recent new age spiritual movements. In the first case, technological and military power tempted evil men to kill in the name of race and culture. In the second case, the incredible wealth generated by science and capitalism corrupted weak men to turn spiritual ideals into money, power, and sometimes even sex.

Against this corruption, the King (or God or the Light of the Self) must take power and reestablish dharma; a new spiritual and moral order based upon the nondualistic moral principles of unconditional love, charity, balance, peace and justice. In reference to the world wars, this has mostly happened with the victory of the Allies over the Nazis. In reference to the corruption of modern spirituality, the struggle is still taking place.

The King in the story leaves the forest and takes control of the country. Slowly, the world moves closer to utopian perfection under His guidance. The rest of the story speaks to events that have not yet happened in the real world, which I believe is the economic flourishing of mankind with the technological help of artificial intelligence, and also greater political and religious unification supported by a radical shift in human consciousness catalyzed by spirituality, meditation, and perhaps psychedelics. Finally, as the centuries pass and with the help of some chaos and suffering, humans will find balance with nature and with each other. A new age of utopian bliss will dawn, and we will all live happily ever after......or so I hope!!!

And now finally, we get to the final and perhaps deepest spiritual message of my story: the immense profundity of choice, of human freedom of will. This truth must be balanced with the fact that the unconscious operates beyond human consciousness, and therefore beyond the freedom of human will. As mentioned, the archetypal power of the Self overpowers the autonomous ego. The Self and collective unconscious guide the ego down life paths devoted to service of the whole. The Self forces self transcendence upon the mystic and yogi. And yet, paradoxically, even though this shallow form of freedom is out of our hands, the divine choice must still be made; whether to align the will of the ego with the desires of the Self, or to ignore the prophetic calling (and this does happen as people become tempted by power and greed) and fall into spiritual darkness as a result.

Just as Jesus resisted the temptation of the devil when he was forty days in the wildness (the devil promised him all of the riches and power over the earth), the inspired human must choose spiritual light over material darkness, and this choice demands the subordination of one's own desires in order to serve the interests of the greater whole. After being gifted the blissful grace of the Self, after entering the heavenly consciousness of God, the mystic must make the choice; whether to stay in heaven out of personal desire or instead leave father heaven for mother earth, thereby bridging the gap between light and dark, forging the unity of opposites by choosing a life of selfless service to mankind.

And of course, the book that the King gives Arsen at the very end (the book that the Self gives to the ego) represents the Paradoxical Light; the book that God wrote through me in order to inspire my dumbass to stop being a dumbass and actually carry out my calling. I left earth for heaven only to come back to earth with a mission; a desire to transform this world into God's most beautiful masterpiece.

This is the final message of the story. It is a paradox. Only the saints can truly find the bliss of God-consciousness. Only those who are willing to give up heaven and selflessly dive into the darkness of this world, alleviating suffering and transferring joy, are the ones gifted the Kingdom of God. The saints will inherit the earth. Heaven on earth, the realization of God, the unity of opposites is the divine plan. It is a fact of oneness woven into the fabric of the universe.

Bonus Chapter Intermission

The ego consciousness of India tends to be so loose that many saints not only experience inflation and alienation from the archetypes, but also union with the archetypes of the Divine Mother and Father through union with the nondualistic Self. The Indian saint sees the Self in all, the one loving source of being, because he has transcended the ego to an incredibly high degree. This is why Sri Ramakrishna went into states of bliss by worshipping the Divine Mother. He would unite into super intoxicated bliss as he merged with the archetype of the Mother by uniting with the nondual archetype of the Self, and slightly less intoxicated bliss when he went back into his very transcendent humble and loving ego. There is very little ego inflation because there is very little ego. There is just love, service, and being a spiritual badness.

The western ego consciousness tends to be denser, although this can be loosened by the safe and spiritual usage of psychedelics. Sex and stimulant drugs make the ego denser (as I can personally attest). The shadow forms with greater power. This creates alienation from the archetypes of the blissful Self and the fall into ego and separation. This is why Satchidananda was a dumbass.

Bonus Chapter Part Deux

"There's got to be a healing of the split between Christ and Satan."

"Christianity tends to have an archetypal split in its concept of evil." -Robert Moore, Jungian Analyst

This healing cannot be achieved so long as the ego remains distinct from the Self. This is why Advaita Vedanta is the solution to this world's problems. You must transcend the body-mind so completely that the Self is almost all there is. This is the nondualistic realization of God, or the One. It is the unity of opposites.

So, what follows is just me thinking as I write. There is a dark side to the Self. This is what happens when archetypes of the Father and (perhaps) Mother are brought down and sexualized. This makes the ego open to possession by dark forces, as the materialism of western culture drives men to perform acts of vile evil;

where the ego is inflated so profoundly that the other does not matter at all.

The solution to this is the radical elevation of consciousness by tapping into the blissful energies of the Mother and Father Saints of India. Ramakrishna was so blissed out that he would often lose consciousness of outer reality and hit the ground. He was so beyond materiality that he never consummated his marriage with Sarada Devi. Anandamayi Ma was so blissfully transcendent that her husband, who would later become her disciple, could not think of having sex with her. Whenever lower thoughts came to him, Anandamayi Ma would turn into Kali and the Divine Feminine.

This is the simplest truth. The dark side of the God is ego, separation, and materiality. The Light Side is unity and love. The Light is the only thing that really exists; it gives birth to the lesser spiritual light connecting ego and Self, and also the darkness separating the dualistic ego from the nondual Self.

Chapter 8

Ego Inflation and

Being Humbled by the Universe

You would think that after writing such a definitive statement about God and love that I would have some sense of purpose; some level of autonomy and ability to resist the darkness of American culture. But as you will see, this did not happen. For many amazing reasons that we are about to discuss, I didn't get the message. I didn't realize that the story you just read was even about me. I had not yet integrated the spiritual experience completely. One psychotic break was not enough. I need to lose it again and more thoroughly this time. The ego inflation of earlier days needed (maybe not needed) to be balanced by yet another wounding, another humbling, a more powerful alienation, and much much more suffering.

Looking back on it, I can't believe that I was so dense. Paradoxically, my abrupt encounter with the Self archetype damaged the connection between my undeveloped ego and the Self, and perhaps (I'm hypothesizing here) a psychotic break needed to happen. This might be because the initial blissful experience of the Self was so deep in the collective unconscious that I needed to break into it consciously for my little ego to figure out what was going on.

People often say the only way out is through. And perhaps this is the case for me. I needed to be consumed by the collective unconscious; I needed to experience the full effects of archetypal divine inflation and the consequent alienation (alienation and inflation are flip sides of the same coin) in order to reestablish connection with the Self, with God.

So as mentioned, the reality of the Self was operating in my life without my conscious awareness or involvement with its aspirations and calling for my life. The ego was still in play because my shadow, which the ego is tied to, was not completely integrated due to my early days of drug addiction. And this deep desire for drugs drove me once again to seek them out; only this time I was much more clever.

Remember, I did not realize that the fantasy story of Arsen and the King was about me. Therefore, my divine calling was not consciously being lived out. Therefore, after some time in the bookstore, I decided to go back to college to become a physical therapist. I liked the college atmosphere, but again, the energy of youth possessed me to go out and get myself prescribed to Adderall.

Initially, the Adderall did not inflate my shadow and, consequently, my ego. But as the weeks went by, I was possessed more and more by this shadow. And since I had already realized the archetype of the Self and even the occasional union with the Self, the shadow and ego inflation had a religious delusional spin to it.

Here it is in a nutshell. I went to California, got super high on drugs, lost my mind to the deepest psychosis that I have ever been in, and thought that I was God. I thought that my ego and my body-mind was God. And here is the crazy thing. Initially, I was God taking over the world, but as the delusion progressed, I realized that I was the only Being in existence. And now, of course, this is complete delusion if you interpret it from the lens of the body-mind-ego. But it is the deepest Truth of the Self. Only God exists. God is the center and circle of everything. God is.

Okay now, here is the longer version of the story............NOTTT! You dear, will have to wait for the second installment of this Jungian series to find out just how crazy shit's gonna get.

Made in the USA
Columbia, SC
12 August 2024